Wild Things

A Color-In Book™
for all ages
Emily Fotis

© 2015 Emily Fotis
All Rights Reserved

Published by Inkstone Arts
P.O. Box 531
Fairfield, Iowa 52556

First Printing

No part of this book may be reproduced by any means, including photocopy, digital imaging, or photo mechanical means, without express written permission of the artist.

Contact the artist: visit emilyfotis.com; emmycat.etsy.com; color-ins.com

ISBN # 978-0-944341-06-3

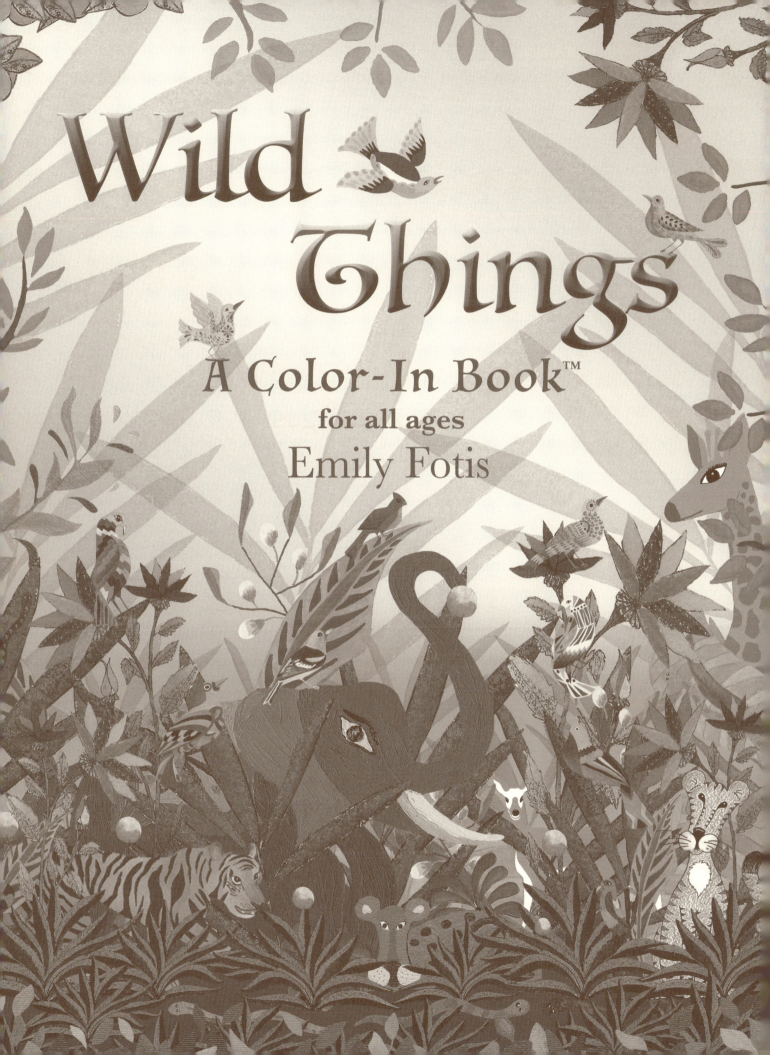

About the Artist

"Go forth, my heart, and seek delight." – Paul Gerhardt, hymn to summertime

Her lifelong delights in nature, color, pattern and fantasy inspire the art of Emily Fotis.

Admirers compare her work to such timeless greats as William Morris, Henri Rousseau, and Laurel Burch – but, Emily's playful, imaginative art is distinctively her own.

Working entirely by hand in various media, Emily creates vibrant originals characterized by her gifts for harmonious color and pattern. Her paintings contain motifs such as birds and other animals, flowers and geometric forms. They range from primitive to refined, from vivid to ethereal – each unique and charming, and each somehow infused with a life and personality of its own.

A self-taught artist, Emily began showing and selling her work in her late teens, starting with her extensive series of paintings inspired by the early Pennsylvania Dutch folk art known as "American Fraktur." For this series, Emily painted on found antique papers, using handmade watercolors prepared from pigment stones that she collected from local creekbeds.

Her shows and sales have created demand for Emily's art beyond paintings and prints. An experienced graphic designer, Emily works with clients to create business logos, advertising materials, package and concept design, CD album design, and book covers. Her first all-ages coloring book was published in 2004. She produces a line of frameable greeting cards, launched in 2006 as *Inkstone Arts Fine Art Frameables*. Emily incorporates her art into stationery, jewelry, journals, housewares and giftware, sold in local shops and at her etsy store, EmmyCat.etsy.com. Emily also licenses her art.

But her greatest delight, by far, is in creating new, original works. Emily likes to experiment with different materials, styles and techniques to expand the scope of her art. In addition to watercolors, she works in oils, gouache, casein and acrylic paints, inks, pencils and markers. (She has also created "paintings" done entirely in blended polymer clays!)

Response to Emily's art has been extraordinary. Viewers young and old, connoisseur and novice, express a remarkably unanimous emotional reaction to her work. Whether they describe the effect as joyful, magical, peaceful, delightful, or inspiring – simply stated, Emily's art makes people happy.

P.S. Emily has often winced at mispronunciations and misspellings of her last name – "Fahtis, Fowtis, Foits, Fortis, Foats" (even, we kid you not, "Fetus" – on a zoo membership card!). So, we thought we'd just clear up the mystery. The original family name was Fotopoulos, shortened when Emily's Greek ancestors came as immigrants to America. **Fotis rhymes with "notice."**

For more information about Emily, her story and her work, visit emilyfotis.com.

About this Book

In the summer of 2003, at her first solo-artist exhibit of her American Fraktur Paintings, Emily set up a painting table where guests could learn to make watercolors and paint the colors on sepia outlines of her drawings. The activity was wildly popular among guests of all ages – many requesting extra outlines to take home to their families. This sparked Emily's love of innovation – she decided to create "the first-ever coloring book that both children and adults can enjoy!"

And as promised, in 2004, Emily's *American Fraktur Paint-and-Color Book* was born. Despite very limited marketing, the book has enjoyed steady sales through the years, earning enthusiastic reviews and solid 5-star ratings. In 2010, the book was chosen by renowned artist and critic Eric Fischl, for inclusion in the gift shop of his traveling, multi-artist exhibit, *America: Now and Here*.

Emily put much thought and care into making that book user-friendly, and into giving buyers something *more* than just temporary fun. After coloring, they would have 18 authentic artworks – to leave in the book (as their own "collected works"), or to remove and give as gifts or decorate their own spaces.

Perhaps that's why her buyers have become her most loyal fans – many buying additional copies as gifts for others, or just for the pleasure of doing it all over again, themselves (maybe even improving on their first efforts). They have long been asking, politely: "*More coloring books, please!*"

And – *ta-da!* – here, at last, is the second in what Emily plans as a series of Color-In Books™ of various themes and styles. It incorporates all the same convenient, user-friendly features and options as her first. Plus, Emily has added a special bonus – at the end of this book, you'll find a sneak preview of her next book (already in the works) – with an outline from that book, large enough to enjoy coloring right now.

So, put on your comfiest clothes; turn off your phones and gadgets and buzzers and beepers; close the door and put out the "Do Not Disturb" sign. Then, relax, enter *the Zone* – and *create*!

Get in Touch

We welcome constructive feedback and/or criticism. If you have any questions, difficulties or suggestions for improvement, please email Kate@InkstoneArts.com. Or write to Inkstone Arts Publications, PO Box 531, Fairfield, IA 52556. For more information about this book and other Color-Ins™ products, visit Color-Ins.com.

We guarantee free replacement of any book received in damaged condition. If your seller does not have a damage replacement policy, contact **CustomerService@InkstoneArts.com** and we'll take care of it.

Naturally, we hope you will love this book and find it fully lives up to our descriptions. We would like to learn about your experiences with these projects and how you're using your finished work. Pictures of completed paintings and/or needlepoint projects would be great, too. To share, like us on Facebook and join our Color-Ins group at http://www.facebook.com/colorinbooks. Enjoy!

Just for fun – see if you can find these on the front cover:
• 6 mammals • 5 reptiles • 11 birds – and find the two birds that aren't in this book!

A Special Note From Emily

I can't remember a time when I didn't love to draw and paint and sculpt and design. My childhood was spent in "messing around" with whatever materials were at hand. The pleasure my creations brought to others was a happy surprise.

I am a self-taught artist – and still learning! When I was 17, I did something that I highly recommend to all aspiring artists: I took instruction from a master calligrapher, to develop line control and line quality. From the same teacher, I learned how to make inks from walnut shells and paints from stones. Then, I started to paint.

I wanted a career in art, but observation taught me that "real" art is supposed to be serious and difficult, for both artist and viewer. However, it's not in my nature to create art that perturbs. Nor did I want to portray objects with photographic precision. I simply wanted to keep doing what I loved.

And what I loved was "folk art" – the innocent, unpretentious, spontaneous art of The People. From ancient cave paintings to illuminated manuscripts to the "naive primitives" of tribal cultures everywhere, people have celebrated life through art. We beautify our dwellings, our garments, our implements and documents, our villages and towns and cities, because it brings us joy. The urge to create is universal.

This book has been some time in the making. I dedicate it here, with heartfelt affection and gratitude, to my loyal (and patient!) friends whose support has allowed me to keep doing the work I love.

My aim is to symbolize the playfulness, exuberance and infinite creativity of Nature. If the viewer senses a message of hope and delight, my aim will have found its mark.

Emily

Get the Most Fun from Your Color-In Books™

For Color-Inners

• <u>Single-sided printing</u> allows full use of every design. This feature also suggests some novel uses for this book: (1) Keep the book intact as your own "collected works" **or** (2) Keep intact & use blank sections as a journal/notebook/sketch pad! To make sure nothing shows through *from either side*, we recommend putting your journal/sketch pages on separate, smaller, lightweight papers & lightly pasting these onto the blank backs. An ideal paste for this is *Yes! Paste*, widely available at art & craft stores/websites.

• <u>Perforated pages</u> – Remove outlines to color or frame. You can use the same *Yes! Paste* to mount your paintings for matting & framing. These make lovely gifts/decoration for your home/office. These paintings are especially appealing to babies & children, so they'd be wonderful in kid-spaces. **NOTE: Some of you may wish to copy outline pages, to try out color schemes before completing the art. Ordinarily, this would violate copyright restrictions. But, Emily wants her buyers to have this freedom. See "Special Express Permissions" below.**

- Ivory paper creates a finished look, makes background color-in optional. Some of the *original paintings* outlined in this book are colored edge-to-edge with no background. Some have uncolored backgrounds, such as the *American Fraktur* series – ivory simulates those antique papers. Most paintings with original background colors look quite wonderful on ivory, as well.

- Sepia colored outlines eliminate intrusive black lines on finished work. Another advantage: sepia outlines let you skip coloring every last leaf, stem & curlicue – or details such as edgings & animal eyes – because sepia is close to some colors in Emily's originals. A great feature for those who don't want to get too fussy!

- Heavy paper suitable for markers, pens, pencils & crayons, and all water-based paints (watercolors, casein, gouache, acrylics). Following are exceptions, caveats & suggestions:
    - Broad-tipped ("fine") **Sharpie®** **brand permanent markers** will bleed through to the underside of the paper: We recommend putting a blank piece of paper behind the outline page, to protect your book/work surface. Other very strong/wet markers will likely bleed through.
    - "Ultra-fine" tipped **Sharpie®** **markers** will show through on the underside, but not *bleed* through.
    - **Sharpie®** claims its pens will not bleed through. In our experience, this is true of all pens.
    - Water-based paints *in a thick, somewhat dry state* work well on this paper. *Very wet paints* may wrinkle or dimple the paper slightly, but in our tests these have not bled through.
    - Acrylic, casein & gouache paints tend to sit on the surface of the paper until dry, and therefore don't bleed through.
    - We do not recommend using oil paints or oils pastels on this paper.

For Needlepointers

Most of the designs in this book make gorgeous needlepoint patterns! Buyers of Emily's first coloring book (*American Fraktur Paint-and-Color Book, 2004*) have asked permission to do this & have loved the results. Emily wants buyers of this book to have the same freedom & fun. See below for special permissions.

Special Express Permissions

- *Emily Fotis hereby grants express permission, limited to original owners of this book (whether owned by purchase or gift) to copy any outline page herein, to try out a color scheme; or to create a needlepoint pattern.**
- *Any copies/patterns created for these purposes are limited to the exclusive use of the original owner only.**
- *Original owners may give finished paintings/needlepoint projects – but NOT copied outlines/patterns – as gifts.**

Any wider distribution and/or sales/commercial use of any outline(s)/pattern(s) herein, by anyone, for any purpose, is forbidden, and will call forth our pack of wild dingos to howl and snarl outside your door.

Color & Media Suggestions

- Full-color thumbnails of all 32 original paintings are included. Sometimes, an outline can be a bit confusing, especially for new colorists – *Where do I begin? What are these little thingamabobs? Why are there some double outlines?* Full-color images can help you identify details, and can serve as a color guide if you wish to use similar colors. They can also guide those who prefer to let their own imagination & color sense come to play. Either way – *you're the artist!*

- These paintings will look best in either bright jewel-tones or natural (but still rich) earthy hues. Pastel colors will not do justice to the art.

- Metallic/pearlescent/iridescent touches can be lovely *in small doses*. Metallics can subtly highlight a few flower or leaf edges, geometric motifs, stars, or sun faces/beams. Birds have naturally iridescent, waterproof feathers, so small strokes of pearlescent or iridescent paints on a wing/back can mimic nature.

Some of our favorite media & brands: • SHIVA Casein Colors • HOLBEIN Irodori Antique Watercolors • SAKURA Pigma® Micron Pens • DERWENT Watercolor Pencils • FABER CASTELL Color Pencils • LUKAS or M. GRAHAM Gouache • TURNER Acryl Gouache • WINDSOR & NEWTON Designer's Gouache (Gold & Silver)

'BURNING BRIGHT' OUTLINE © 2015 EMILY FOTIS

'KALEIDOSCOPE' OUTLINE © 2015 EMILY FOTIS

'LABYRINTH' OUTLINE © 2015 EMILY FOTIS

'BEAUTY IN THE BEASTS' OUTLINE © 2015 EMILY FOTIS

'BIRD'S-EYE VIEW' OUTLINE © 2015 EMILY FOTIS

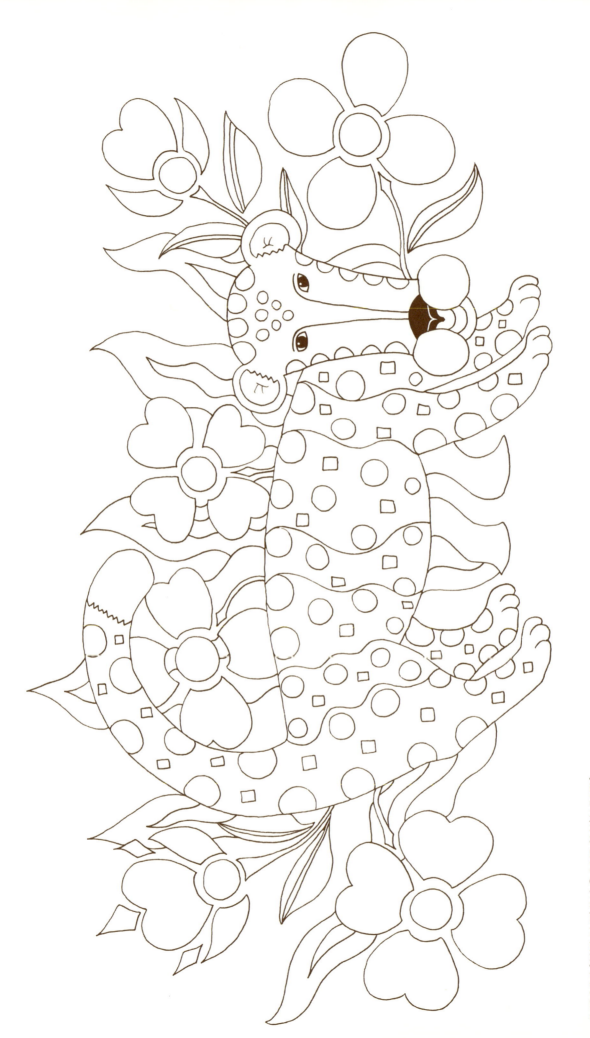

'GEOBIRD' OUTLINE © 2015 EMILY FOTIS

Sell your books at sellbackyourBook.com!
Go to sellbackyourBook.com
and get an instant price
quote. We even pay the
shipping - see what your old
books are worth today!

Inspected By: Santiago_Torres

0004924683

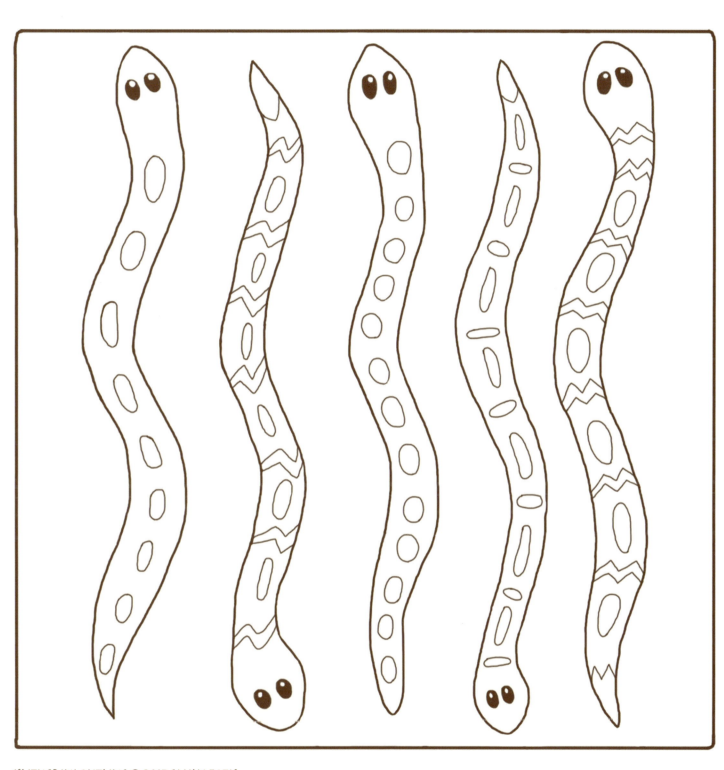

'SLITHERIN' OUTLINE © 2015 EMILY FOTIS

'DOE WITH FAWN' OUTLINE © 2015 EMILY FOTIS

'SERENITY' OUTLINE © 2015 EMILY FOTIS

'PURPLE-THROATED SHARPIE' OUTLINE © 2015 EMILY FOTIS

'TAPESTRY' OUTLINE © 2015 EMILY FOTIS

'CARDINAL' OUTLINE © 2015 EMILY FOTIS

'LITTLE GEM' OUTLINE © 2015 EMILY FOTIS

'CAROUSEL' OUTLINE © 2015 EMILY FOTIS

Special Sneak Preview of Coming Attractions!

Old Playful's Book of Impractical Cats
& other Curious Critters

A Copious Collection of Cattitude!

- All new Color-In Art Outlines in a variety of styles • Same great user-friendly features
- Projected release in mid-2016 • Check for updates at www.Color-Ins.com

Meanwhile, here's *Sabrina*, The World's Sweetest Kitty, who has graciously offered herself for your coloring pleasure right now. Please be gentle – she's a bit ticklish!